the flap pamphlet series

Yellow Things: A Family Operetta

open, read, turn

Yellow Things: A Family Operetta

the flap pamphlet series (No. 30)
Printed and Bound in the United Kingdom

Published by the flap series, 2025
the pamphlet series of flipped eye publishing
All Rights Reserved

Cover Design by Petraski
Series Design © flipped eye publishing, 2010

Author Photo © Deven Philbrick
First Edition
Copyright © **Caroline Fernelius** 2025

The first iterations of *Prelude, Yellow Things* and *Saturn devours his Son* appeared in Storyscape Journal's Summer 2020 issue.

An earlier iteration of *A: Another Biography* appeared in Wax Nine Journal's January 2022 issue.

Yellow Things: A Family Operetta was named a finalist in the Wax Nine 1st Annual Chapbook Contest in December 2021.

ISBN-13: 978-1-905233-81-6

Yellow Things:
A Family Operetta

Caroline Fernelius

"Yellow? said Geryon. And he was thinking Yellow! Yellow! Even in dreams he doesn't know me at all! Yellow!"
— Anne Carson, *Autobiography of Red*

"Operetta is a form of theatre and a genre of light opera. It includes spoken dialogue, songs, and dances. It is lighter than opera in terms of its music, orchestral size, length of the work, and at face value, subject matter. Apart from its shorter length, the operetta is usually of a light and amusing character. It sometimes also includes satirical commentaries."
— Wikipedia, "Operetta"

For Baba half-dust woman

Contents | *Yellow Things: A Family Operetta*

Prelude 9
Yellow Things 10
Saturn devours his Son 14
Atonement 17
An Interlude 18
Yellow Things 20
Saturn devours his Son 22
Atonement 24
K: A Biography (and interludes) 25
A: Another Biography 32

Prelude

A priori:
I have to tell the story of my sister's rape and my mother's succumbing (to
what? All that I can say is that it was like quicksand; December in the south of Texas takes
no pore
for granted)

Theorem A:
If I tell the story of my sister's rape and my mother's succumbing then I am the exploiter
(i.e. taking something that isn't mine) my sister once told me I could make anything
sound pretty it seems like a compliment it was not one
And since then I have been trying to court ugliness in places more expansive than
the gulf of Mexico   In March for example
a Korean café in Providence, Rhode Island   over a plate of orange foods a man told me he
was working on a dissertation about Gertrude Stein and the grotesque   I did not ask
him to elaborate   I want to make things ugly ugly ugly I wish I could
do that.

Theorem A, in translation:
If I tell the story of my sister's rape and my mother's succumbing then I will do
unforgivable things like talk about Hephaistos and Athena in a story about my sister's rape
and my mother's succumbing.

Theorem B:
If I do not tell the story of my sister's rape and my mother's succumbing then for the rest
of my life I will make things that obliquely refer to the thing which I wanted to explain
I wanted to explain denial and so I wrote my senior thesis on nuns
I wanted to explain food and so I studied the holy communion in excruciating detail
I wanted to explain sex and I did not understand the question.

If I do not tell the story of my sister's rape and my mother's succumbing then   I will ignore
letters and fridges for all time   their slippery fluorescence mocking
an utter inability to commit. To put down the fact that December in Florida is strikingly
similar in both meter and tone   I want to make things ugly ugly ugly I wish I could
do that.

Yellow Things

I.

I love geometry class the little rules I copy in my own book the boy in front calls me ginger
I am not one copying rules go home to the dogs
Penny and Owen   go to my room copying more rules making things.

When I was young I wore my hair in a ponytail and discovered one could not make things
with words always if one wanted to refrain from turning into dust   completely
My grandmother half-dust woman puts colors and mud-caked coins into my hands I put
them in rows I cannot become all dust   just yet my mother
she's all clay, downstairs telling brother
stop making a mess with that rice blue bowl for me on
the stovetop she relishes in making us things cruel indirect   object.

These are round days made of Graham Cracker crust hand lotion swingset in neighbor's
yard I go there to think
Come home for chicken cutlets seared in butter and mother's thin wrists waving over
tomato coulis with mint   I yell at my brothers they yell at me my mother
puts sister's hair at the top of her head she's all pink goes
to a studio downtown to make lines for hours I stay
think of her lines at night flip the pillow to the cool side

Shh shh sh sh sh ah.

II.

These were days with no edges chocolate pudding in biodegradable cups my mouth
bubbling over with words I put them in
my small notebooks and mail grandmother half-dust woman a copy

In English class. When you grow up on the wrong side of relevant every window reveals
Texas southwestern sky gas station with a man who sells Bahn mí sandwiches they sell out
every morning at eleven down below
well I am staring out that window when my teacher says there's a lot you don't know.

For example I once got engaged to a woman she left I sold the car went to England taught
literature in a small town you wouldn't know it either   I say all this to say oh I don't
know sometimes we just like to tell stories you get it   right turn
the page I write in my short response that one day I will go away too this
revelation receives an A+   hair down to my elbows at fourteen and I have managed to make
the east coast of America countercultural its steeples and
squares and everything the people there made of edges and corners
during the round days I dream in terms of breakfast with my father on the Charles
this revelation receives an A+   and sister is still in the studio downtown making lines she is
supple and infantile they
are not are never.

For my final paper I write an essay about circles.
My teacher puts it on the wall my mother shakes her head in
astonishmentwonderdisgust says I don't know where you got it I   didn't make you.

III.

In world history class Castor pressed a pencil eraser to my left shoulder
blade I did not expect to find him among ancient Chinese warfare and those
goddamn southwestern windows he gave
a note it said *meet me outside the auditorium 4 pm* I went with my hair to my
elbows his greaser jacket caught in left hand dragging the cement below I think this
is the point of parallelism when we kissed I thought of round unknowable things
for days my mother by the sink back-turned who's that boy in the back
he's my friend well she says I never had a friend like that in my life.

Upstairs his tar hair in my hair   the Gulf Coast
in March takes no pore for granted we make jokes
about the imaginary radiator and Castor he is trying to be a man.

IV.

A woman has instructed her assistant to take photographs as she
climb climb climbs a steel spiked ladder at the contemporary art museum

All line and edge where did a girl of twelve learn all that where did she ingest it where is
the beginning of the thread I ask demanding

Castor frowns he thinks we are talking about different things I ask him what difference
means he gestures towards the blood on the assistant's shin there it is I would never
puncture my skin for the beginnings and the endings of things it's a kind of self-indulgence
I stop him there

At home in bed Castor is licking his thumb while downstairs my sister is learning how
good it feels to say no she will say it for a very long time all girl and edge and line floating
somewhere in the stratosphere of round and rounding days

When come nighttime sitting round a wooden table I realize I eat like a boy
my brothers and dad and me bread fish fried onions fingers digging around in our mouths
like steel hooks and sister and mother sit side by side whispering
I say what are you talking about mother says nothing eat your rice how about you eat some
rice I'm done here well so are we your sister doesn't feel good yeah well she doesn't look
good neither and as it turns out round days dissolve in the darkness
and I am still trying to figure out how lines and
edges both take up and eliminate space
maybe that's why sister pushes her plate mother follows wordless I call Castor
I want to make things ugly ugly ugly I tell him I wish I could
do that.

V.

In Texas that summer we were drunk on sun the whole time me and Castor taking
roundness and running with it like we were getting away with
something cackling the whole way down I-45 in my red car I felt like there was too much
inside of me for sixteen I said Castor do you ever feel like there's too much *no* he goes
look at the billboards I think billboards are so sad well okay Castor.

Get off at the grocery store on Green Boulevard   talk about   atoms drink orange juice Castor
I say   have you ever wanted to be so small   he doesn't answer he says
when you look at the sun like that *jesus christ your eyes* well
I have always wanted to be beheld   the way you behold and I know you have a
general   distaste for the beginnings and endings of things but I think that's it
right there

VI.

Across from Houstonian bay windows I realize I am eating for three
Mom I say have you ever   thought there was too much inside no she says I don't know
what you mean and if I did my answer would still be no she takes a laboratory flask of
chardonnay to the lips ah she says that's   better

Mom I say do you remember the toast days   what she says her torso unmoving hand still
gripping   the base of an afternoon white the toast I tell her you used to eat it in your
pajamas   on this stool here fried egg with a crack of   pepper on top like confetti
with restraint do you recall the toast days she says go get your brothers   dinner's ready.

13

Saturn devours his Son

I.

Mother was right it was hell dreaming backwards
me fingering without alarm or regard the dorm room radiator I always thought
I wanted and Cassius on the line like *sorry babe I just have a different
concept of time I guess*
In the morning we eat orange things for breakfast   when Mom rings from
the South I am in love with how far away I feel *now why would you do this to
yourself I didn't raise a shrinking violet* she says *is he really that good*

On the bench outside the music
library dark heat to rival Gulf Coast waters
in October *it's a shame* says Cassius
what is *just your brain you're so smart but it's all poisoned* I take
one look at Carolina oak delicate and ever expanding beneath
east coast moon   well you know boy I remember everything

Cassius is foreign to me I breathe to mother later in the state that is half slumbering
half wanting   boys who know the beginnings and endings of things are
foreign to me he worships edges and lines he wishes to gather and roll
around in them for an eternity I do not know what to do with all of that sharpness *be calm*
she says *see how it goes* when it ends I nearly dissolve in rage think of Saturn
devouring his Son for months.

II.

After the yellow things sister learns again the retreat   and mother telling me on the phone
*she'd like to hear from you you know it's like you're better at loving her
from afar* oh I go well the words went and ran out I can't write her into anything
anymore I tried that   when I tried   my own words lysed like I was back in freshman year
biology   I ate sawdust for weeks   I guess I wanted to see what it was like
to wage that kinda war so don't go asking me for words because mine they went and
ran out

III.

In the absence of round days we poured helium into the crevices behind and between
our radiators talked about hometowns over Italian on Broad St you know
I think that I'm from here now I eat my dinners from a carton box and it feels
right leaving the library past twilight I wrote the last line of Wallace Stevens' "Gray Room"
in every notebook they no longer contain the little geometric rules but all night I
am trying to make things did I tell you the boy in my Whitman class has the voice of God
Father calls

talks about the flies at night and the heat a watercolor dripping Texan erudition brisket
supper the whole thing like a wet wet dog in mourning. Everything's good papa.

IV.*

V.*

VI.*

VII.

In the moment when all became perpendicular I was alone in darkness waiting for a place
to put my dirty dish on the conveyor belt washing machine I saw him and I knew I knew
I knew

Hello can you help me I did not have words for after that what he says his curls
chiseled marble I'd follow you to Japan if you asked (I thought but did not say)
well alright then he replies
in the moment when all became   perpendicular I was hungry for weeks my thumb was
half the size of his I told him I will remember our thumbs comparatively speaking for
the rest of my days I will Ajax I will

---

*Ten seconds

15

VIII.

My sister is making mudcakes in the jungle Ajax comes
over in the darkening heat of August says *what's for breakfast* not mudcakes!
no I'm making lists over here
and if you sit still for a second I may never let you leave
well then how would I do this now huh at the beach his hands half dust I think of stars
how they are
geometrically improbable
how he is always trying to approach my words in similar fashion
you see he says gently *you need proof for that*

I see your point (lying)

his half dust hands commanding seasalt air touching cloud touching me

IX.

Funny how you can love something that unseeing I'd
return to him over and over I do return to him
over and over I read every line peruse every crease
in a seminar I write an essay about this phenomenon of the unseeing
email it to mother who replies after exactly one hour and seven minutes:
wow need to read it over again something not making sense but wow
your sister is doing well in her letters discusses the flora and the fauna
and currently constructing a written autobiography before bedtime—

Atonement

When Hephaistos tried to take Athena she scraped off his seed with a piece of wool sent
it flinging towards the ground accidentally impregnated the earth and a child begot with
serpent scales for a body

when Athena's sisters saw it they threw themselves off the Acropolis or else were killed by
the child-serpent the ancient writers can't agree and I have spent hours days weeks *say it*
years trying to write you into wellness it's true Whitman thought he could save the nation
with his verse he thought the poetic I a thing divine he thought he thought he spent a life
thinking and they still

went and did it his pages went limp under layers of sawdust and as for me I tried
to make things so beautiful you would agree to stay you would agree to eat chocolate
slowly you would agree to look at the men on the subway golden strands of hair parting
and coalescing in equal measure every time and I would give up rage I would cut
out words and put them in little envelopes and give them all away I would worship
at the feet of everything purple instead I would I would I
would

***

Theorem B my friend tells me over tea *Theorem B B B*
At first I do not recall my own words he says again *Theorem B* if you do not tell the story of
your sister's rape and your mother's succumbing then for the rest of time you will obliquely
refer to the thing which you wanted to explain:

You wanted to explain denial and so you wrote about geometry
You wanted to explain food and so you pontificated somewhat unintelligibly
about sawdust and the female form
You wanted to explain sex and still you did not understand the question.

I thought I'd done it I say irate discussed the beginnings and the endings articulated the
consequences of the Gulf Coast I thought I could say the thing without saying
My friend interjects—Remember Cassius' poem?
Cassius?
Part B Cassius
oh yes I see
He wrote a poem said it was about you but it wasn't really it was about a man on a ship
who searched for gold until eventually he died get it? it wasn't about you at all
but he thought he really really thought
oh
yes uncanny right

I didn't realize we had so much in common

*

In truth this friend of mine has always urged continual returnings.
He gave me a copy of Tom McCarthy's *Remainder* last fall when my heart (Ajax) was
undergoing a piecemeal splintering

in the novel the main character repeatedly buys cappuccinos at the coffee shop he is trying
to get punches in his card to receive a free cappuccino in so doing he becomes enamored
of the process of ordering he buys five six seven cappuccinos drinks

them all in the reviews online they call this writing laborious (huh) but I think it is the best part of the entire book I think about cappuccinos for a long time splintering heart and all.

So let me begin again.

* * *

Yellow Things

I.

I tell him: when I say that things were yellow I mean that me and sister wore matching bows we had small dolls the size of our own fingers each morning making a house in which the dolls might live but when the house was finished I crept hungry and alone back down the stairs

Dad smoking hot dogs in November I think we were still quite small when we realized she was beautiful this sounds like a blessing it is not one during the yellow times we saw in sun drenched film how beauty was sin the people always dying or almost dying *hold up* he says go on I reply not not irritated *what about your father* what about my father I told you he was the king of round   lines never had a chance with him *you're ignoring something* it isn't important *if you're ignoring it it is* ah.

II.

My father was born in Ohio his father before him didn't say much
the first sixty or so years of his life and now he can't stop his words foam at the mouth much like mine do but anyway my father was born in Ohio to a teacher and a tax accountant he ran around the flatlands at night biked to the corner store bought popsicles thought about redheaded girls in the morning went to school thought to himself I have to get out of here there is nothing wrong but I have to get out of here he never said this to his folks and when the letter came from the East they looked at him three times said I didn't make you

Out East is where the wanting first began jogging around the monuments at night in the stillness he decided to eat everything there was to eat law firm recruitment receptions women in sheer skirts the Honduran Embassy and bacon grease come morning

Ah my friend says *interesting* how so *the unseeing* the unseeing *An incurable blindness if you will* how so *he was the king of round lines never had a chance with him he decided to eat everything there was to eat law firm recruitment receptions women in sheer skirts*

the Honduran Embassy bacon grease come morning he never stopped did he he never stopped right *and your sister the beautiful one* uh huh *she is sitting there making lines and eating sawdust* right *right.*

III.

Thinking now over tea I realize Castor is no Hades he walked around my kitchen with a wooden spoon he gave my brother a red boxcar wrapped in handkerchief I gave him many things and he was continuously returning them to me unscathed it was a ritual I could not respect I tried and when I was done trying I tried again *yes* says my friend what now *she really did make you*

Saturn devours his Son

I.

In North Carolina everything was ensconced in a technicolor sheath we drank blue liquid in thin paper cups that fell over when we blew on them the sky was a deepening orange I didn't see morning for some number of months when mother called and asked if I was happy I said *no I'll never leave the frat houses on Broad St contain multitudes and I never want to leave*

When my sister started to give things back (her will as well as the tiny elephant figurines atop her nightstand she gave away worrying she gave away that feeling you get when you are sure about something she gave away tennis shoes spent gum wrappers little glasses with tulips hand-painted on the sides an I heart NY t-shirt she gave away grace she gave away the entirety of the New Testament she gave away colors shoestrings dishwasher soap she gave away disagreeing she gave away scarves embroidered with her own name she gave away socks she gave away vodka in thin little tubes) when she was giving all this away

I became beholden to the idea that I could take everything I took paperclips I took money I took condoms I had no intention of using I took shards from the glass-stained windows up at the Divinity School I took love I took chocolate bunnies wrapped in gold tinfoil I took my memories of 9/11 I took scotch tape and expired library cards and baked Amish oatmeal I took my ideas concerning Wallace Stevens' appropriation of American jazz I took illegible sheets of music I took the hurricane of 1900 I took shot glasses I took Aperol liqueur I took boys in gray winter hats I took a public policy studies textbook I took the entire southwestern stretch of I-84 I took and I took and I took and it was never close to enough I took until the taking ran out

II.

He licks his lips   slowly *this is about him isn't it* I don't know what you are saying
*for the rest of your days you will make things which obliquely refer to the thing you wanted
to explain* but Ajax *there it is* he took something
that belonged to me I will spend an eternity trying

to get it back *that isn't true* that isn't true I gave him something of my own volition
I gave him many things I will spend an eternity trying to get them back *what did you give* seasalt I gave seasalt *what else* I gave him that look on my face when I've just figured something out *and* I gave him cutout comic strips a squat glass bottle of orange vitamins stripped wine bottles filled with flowers a shower cap three tiny blue bowls an electric teapot my at times crippling insecurity re: the shape of my cheeks how they balloon when I smile how I am consistently not-smiling in photographs as a result a forest green cardigan two envelopes and seven stamps I gave him the recipe for pistachio-crusted salmon I gave him three containers of horchata I gave him my misguided attempts to be better I gave him calendars of years past as part of an inside joke I gave him little poems I gave him toast I gave him every eyelash blown from my knuckles I was prepared to give all of these things and more for a long time possibly *no don't say it*
I was prepared to give all of these things and more and when he left it all became sawdust I put it in my hair and in my teeth and behind the dresser drawers and then I went to sleep.

Atonement

When Hephaistos tried to take Athena she scraped off his seed with a piece of wool sent it flinging towards the ground accidentally impregnated the earth later a child begot with serpent scales for a body when Athena's sisters saw it they threw themselves off the Acropolis or else were killed by the child-serpent the ancient writers can't agree and I am just now starting to understand repetition how in an act of desperation or hubris or something I sought to tell a single story how I was condemned am condemned in that moment to repeat repeat repeat so here is a list of the things I wrote instead:

a dissertation on the color yellow the story of my first time a botched rendering of a misremembered Greek myth the sudden and inescapable desire to fall asleep for a very long time the instantiation of obsession the highways down in North Carolina how they are continuously going and returning in a manner which makes me envious to the point of dissolution the first day of October a boy whose chiseled marble curls I will recall for the remainder of my days my father in Ohio his father before him barely spoke for sixty years now he cannot stop I dreamed a million and one dreams about Florida in December and when the millionth and first was over I dreamed them all over again—

K: A Biography

I.

She was born in November a fine enough month for it all to begin I suppose and when she came her mother initiated scandalously a prayer
She said *god almighty don't let harm come to this child wrap up the arrows the sorrows intended for her with a single scarlet-colored string and give them all to me* he responded he said I will I will I will and when the carriage came home she remembered that when god came to her he was wearing yellow   dastardly yellow the color surprisingly of death always inconceivable (always perhaps a dream)   and when she remembered this she wept and when she wept the baby wept and so they wept together   probably for the first time and everything even the wallpaper in the foyer was all yellow

Her (the baby)'s father up above puzzlingly dark hands gripping dirt red awning he made no bargain with god like the mother did but he had a plan the plan was to paint in the evenings after work eating all there was to eat he made valleys peaks crescendos he put the little girl on his lap said we could
live there you know pointing if you ever want or need we could live there you know

And the little girl laughed and laughed and said nothing and in the evenings the mother made schnitzel they   the mother and father looked at the child together the father looked three times to be exact regarded the yellow outer ring of the girl's iris with astonishmentwonderdisgust said I didn't make her

And the mother and the father the both of them laughed some more and then they agreed that it all made sense anyway because back then everything was all yellow

the linen cabinets and the lunchbox and the tiny modules of sweat that inundated the mother's face when she waking   was confronted with the force of the thing which she had made and feeling the breath of the father on the wet of her neck went back to sleep and dreamed of her dealings with god a god who also wore yellow (the mother did not know if god always wore yellow or simply happened to have on that particular ensemble when visiting her that day in the hospital. Sometimes in waking she hungry for thought enveloped god's frail body in cerulean blue an image which kept her until morning)

But in the morning the rage began a rage which was not loud but ground pulsingly quiet

The child (the girl) inconsolable in her white dress and yellow braids they never did know what was the matter and the child (the girl) recalled at a later time how back then the walls in their yellowness hurt in a way that she (the child) felt would surely kill her
I was raging against a color she said   matter of factly her braids consisting of an ever so slightly increasing number of strands

The mother of course became irate *beautiful and wise* she whispered to the father hands frozen in front fixing things painting mountains *beautiful and wise* she whispered again Her surprise at god for breaking his word lasted all of one moment she went upstairs ran a single finger along the dust that had collected beneath the white oak coffee table and then she went to sleep.

* * *

Already I have betrayed the project

But you just began

In retrospect everything matters which is also the fundamental tragedy of woman

And of the novel

I am not in the business of writing novels I am only trying to keep the tips of my fingers from dragging obstinate   across the keyboard

You know what the solution is

I do not

Put it this way you must take her out of time

Time is a precondition of my belief

How so

* * *

II.

She makes it you know. An anticlimactic ending but an ending nevertheless. I see her on the
internet where she streams chicken coops live from the hills of England hills which
I for one never knew existed
And she has taken to pressing (trapping) dried summer flowers between bits of ombre glass
tokens she then sells at marginal profit   the box containing each one outfitted with a hand
written note
I love you thank you so much for your purchase and her hair by both fortune and intent is no
longer predominantly a shade of yellow   a fact that the mother unceasing comments on
during their daily transcontinental video calls
You've got so much red in you she says surprised she thinks of the girl baby at the house
on Hillswick the bits of golden twine on the child's head furling and unfurling in the
kind of heat that takes everything (even the idea of itself) and she is mad at the father on
behalf of the girl baby the father who scandalized by his own image regarded fried onion a
finger food and spent years typing and then backspacing   riotous questions into his search
engine of choice which formed unwittingly an archive of deletions that said everything

How could you do this to her she said (wanting) it was a Tuesday in September he had
spent the afternoon running background checks on strangers childhood enemies the cashier
at the bodega in Washington who gave him free milk in his coffee nearly every morning
until one day the bodega closed without warning cashier nowhere to be found skipped
town he supposed wordlessly made it out for Antigua a joke it seemed at first but then he
began to believe it

And when he believed it he started to believe other things too wild things irreparable things
he began to believe that each word he printed on the page exhibited right away signals of
distress symptoms of its own internal combustion on top of this though he believed words
were constantly running off the page within the span of a moment (he would go to refill
his mug with coffee and come back to his desk and when he got there he would count how
many words he still had and almost always the number was lower by one or two when

compared to the number he had had only seconds prior)

All of course a long way to say that he didn't get to write her but she (the girl child) forgave him and the mother said she didn't know if she could but she did eventually and no one knew it but it was all thanks to his hands
which   observing one cold morning
she saw anew.

* * *

There's a shoddy realism about it

An attention to each compartment is how I'd phrase it

I am only trying to put her back together

You what

Perhaps I misspoke I'm trying to gather her in unforeseen combinations inelegant sacrilegious even but basically good combinations with blood

I think I have an idea

Oh

The animals

The animals?

The animals

* * *

III.

When I take her out of time there are rabbits everywhere. Rabbits in pinkish white hues
nearly translucent the hundreds of them underneath a nameless bridge in central Texas
perhaps (cheating) but there underneath the nameless bridge she (out of time
which of course means out of body) tends to them the rhythms of her breathing (bygone)
fossilized in the sunflowers and she tends to them and it is good

The sound of the wind like a lonely old man scratching at his beard and the rabbits in their
waiting (a waiting that is somehow I do not know how also outside of time) bring their
rabbit bodies close together
Not for warmth (remember central Texas) but for an idea long forgotten they put
their bodies together and then they wait for an arrival predetermined and yet
somehow barely imagined

Still. It is clear why she had to be the one to come her bodilessneess a precondition for
all bodily concern it seems she wraps their small torsos in linen blankets removes
burrs and mangled clots of wood from their opera house ears and in parting offers the
discarded remains of corn cobs like votive offerings to the temple of yellow

their hind legs quickening in anticipation and the bridge still nameless.

IV.

She found it in the bathtub. It hurt when she pressed up against it and when she took her
fingers to it it was softer than she'd guessed disc-like very flexible the sort of thing one
uncovers and immediately retreats from
the bathwater drained of all color and the little brass clock by the door a determination of
when she might tell the others   carefully partially the girl child filled
suddenly then with images of cotton candy boys passed out in a meadow of
confectionary pink dirty hair funfetti spangled an incomprehensible dream if
there ever was one and the girl child let out a gasp and then she got out of the tub

Mother out front eating egg and toast the cracked pepper on top like confetti with restraint
(you might even say her wrists were made for the task) and when she saw the girl child she
knew she knew she knew

And yet did not say *I have been waiting for you* or *This comes at no surprise* or even *I have no interest in preternatural but predetermined events*

In point of fact she said nothing at all finished her egg and toast the cracked pepper on top and only then did she gather as if from the pulse of day a response

Go put your clothes on and the girl child did as she was told but as for her she never quite forgave the mother (for what she never knew) until one day the tips of her fingers forgot everything
and she was glad.

V.

Inside of a house with red wooden trim and lazily sketched windows a cat hungry and loyal lays out the little decapitated bodies of mice before its human and the human feeling at once honored discovers the truth in a single misplaced whisker. The trouble is that there lies at the center of this drama a lacuna in the lexicon used to describe it. (What now is the cat? Predator? Protector? Poor pathetic product of human manipulation?)

I am still worried that after all this I have managed to write out how much I love you.

VI.

When I take her out of time there is a levee and atop the levee a gravel walkway that (she began to suspect suddenly desirously) led nowhere
And when she began to suspect on this singular occasion she initiated unwittingly what came to be known as the era of suspicion itself
During which she a crown of poppy seeds at the hairline began to suspect other things too wild things irreparable things she suspected that the Declaration of Independence had been fabricated in its entirety a scam of the highest order drawn up in the middle of the night by a precocious student and they (she shuddered to think who) paid him in cronuts for his trouble and he laughed and laughed and only later (in the light of unidirectionally unraveling time) did he realize the gravity of what he had done took his shoes off by the Delaware River and offed himself right then she suspected too in an unrelated fashion that the mother lived a life unseen ate bags of discounted Halloween candy in the early minutes of waking minutes when she not a mother licked her fingers between

and took the bathrobe off the hook on the door and in enveloping
became something else entirely a woman a traitor a savant and descending the stairs took everything there was to take (she took all of the fireflies in the state of Maryland the year of 1981 boys in thin paper mache suits)
At which point in the unmaking she (not the mother) ignited her most daring suspicion yet thought the world little more than a plastic tub of half congealed fruit salad and then she went to sleep.

* * *

This is what you have to say to her this is what you give

You have to understand I wanted at first to write to nobody (impossible) but nobody grew fangs orange tufts of fur a tortoiseshell monocle no bigger than a dime. I had no choice

No choice! No choice! Your voice is an abomination

I never endeavored to make a muse of my mother

If you want to give her something give a summary a raison d'être in the form of a grocery list anything with opposable thumbs

We are barreling towards the end aren't we

So be it. What you must give is something to eat

* * *

A: Another Biography

I.

Strange now to think of you while I walk on the sunny pavement of the arcade
winter in Michigan clear winter noon and I've been up all night, talking, talking, reading Walt
Whitman aloud listening to Miles Davis blues shout blind on the phonograph
the rhythm the rhythm and your cold cracked hands in my head as I barreled through
the triumphant stanzas aloud and wept realizing how we suffer*

Ten o'clock in Mexico City and I cannot get over Allen Ginsberg and the boys on the metro
how they fan their blue legs in the heat one after the other an accordion of youth
and attraction spelling sex Texan oil reserves the fine print of becoming and you mommy
waiting in the south for what hand gripping pollen soaked table and picking alternately at
the cuts at the knee purple radiance your eyes trained on the back door (for what)
and thinking now of San Antonio of bars with green plastic awnings and the shootout you
stopped by virtue of your very red hair (you said and I said)

Dear mommy, I did something bad but I did it for you took an antique hatchet to the woods
behind my house destroyed in a singular motion the notion of Midwestern Americana took
it to bat with my coffee hands and then it was Sunday and I rested
And then it was Monday and I rested some more

(Strange then to think of you in Bologna my ears swollen from a trip to the supermarket
prepaid phone card back on the apartment desk and black heroin alley on the way back)

Strange then to think of you in Paris my collar coming undone on the Rue de Rivoli and a
yellow haired woman on the television baring her tiny pink breasts
my copy of Lucien Febvre's *Life in Renaissance France* an omen you returned unread
(O mother I should have known)

Strange then to think of you in Boston my hair short and wet in February snow
dairy-free artisanal ice creams by the bay and a post-it note you Fedexed to my hotel

---

*Allen Ginsberg, "Kaddish" (1957-1959)

containing simply an equation
Read this you wrote and I wrote in response surely

Strange then to think of you in Durham the hair on the back of my knees dampening
and yelling Ghost in the basement of the social sciences building   the fire
escape up top structurally unsound a metonym for glory and the heating unit drip drip
dripping itself into fugitivity the opposite (not the undoing) of sound

Strange then to think of you in Charleston (on this I have nothing else to say)

Strange then to think of you in New York piss drunk at the Gramercy Park Hotel and my
dying conviction that red velvet curtains could save the world   plush negotiators of time
and space that bind and bend my companion said no
so I hailed the first cab I could get the entirety of Lexington Ave a single brush stroke then
of steelredsteel (scrambled city) seven o'clock in the morning and I felt the tail end of tipsy
triumphant really fucking sad for the crows (this was the first time I had ever really thought
about them)

Strange even to think of you in Cambridge
o holy, holy night

Strange to think of you in LA sad sad city city of duende city of hysteria-born sugarspun
centerpieces and the ink
the ink leaking everywhere Huntington Beach with its freaks and the fire hydrants
stomping out all dissent across the rues and the boulevards
(A mortal city revealed then in the string of drunken tail lights across from the Hollywood
Hotel)

Mother mother, they should have known. Dipped their work boots in sheeps' butter and
thought the holy land more than idea only gave it more than idea only gave it their coins
their cracked craftsman hands thick vials even of their wives' menstrual blood took a
hatchet to go and you don't need me to tell you that when they got there everything
was all yellow.

Acknowledgments

Indescribable thanks to my editor, Lana Hughes, for the kind of attentive & sustained reading poets dream of — I am grateful you deemed Yellow Things worthy of some kind of an audience, but I am even more grateful for the careful devotion that followed. Courtesy of Simone Weil: "Attention is the rarest and purest form of generosity."

Thank you to Emery Jenson, a once-frequent interlocutor and a forever friend. You are everywhere in this little book. And to Lizzy Pott, at whose kitchen counter I first began typing this manuscript, and to whose kitchen counter I am always somehow longing to return.

Thank you to Joseph Donahue and Thomas Ferraro, who, in quite distinct ways, first made me take this all very seriously. Your attention, too, was the rarest gift.

To Deven, inexorably.

www.ingramcontent.com/pod-product-compliance
Lightning Source LLC
Chambersburg PA
CBHW031508040426
42444CB00007B/1261